SPIRITS *of* AMERICA

Brownstone Institute
Austin, Texas
2025

ISBN Paperback: 9781630693015
ISBN Ebook: 9 9781630693008

Published by Brownstone Institute 2025

Interior Art by Afshin Amini
Design by Vanessa Mendozzi

SPIRITS *of* AMERICA

On the Semiquincentennial

JEFFREY TUCKER

BROWNSTONE
INSTITUTE

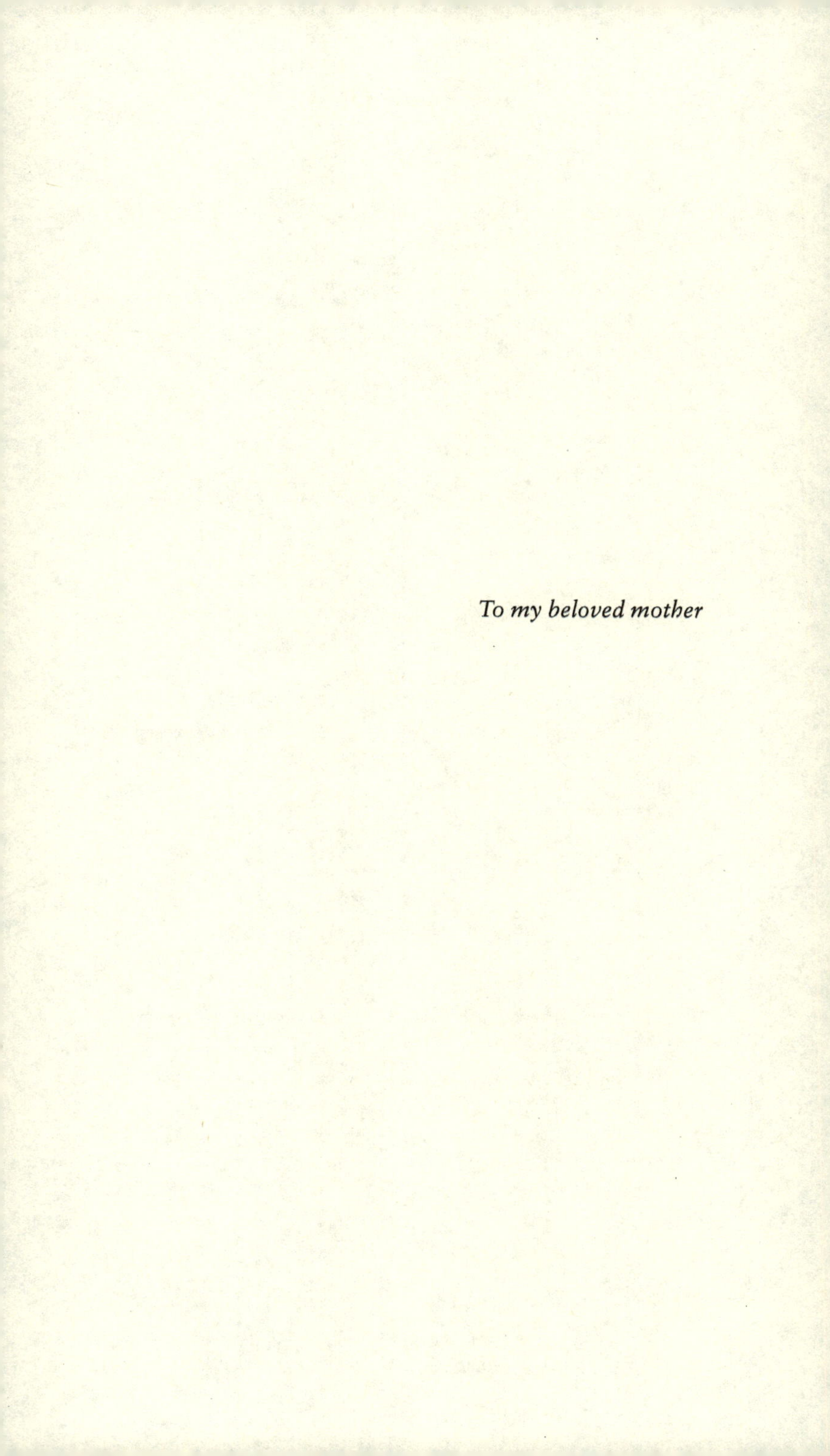

To my beloved mother

Contents

PREFACE

This small book follows two previous books written in full rage against the lockdowns that wrecked life and liberty in 2020 and following. The battles are not over but it seems time to reflect more deeply on larger themes. An angry life is not a good life. We need to rally around that which we love. These years have tempted us all to forget this.

A friend pressed a monograph in my hands by Eric Sloane, an American legend in historiography and illustration, the voice that nearly invented what is called "Americana." The title is *The Spirits of '76*, published in 1973. It is not in print and likely won't be again. As it turns out, this is Sloane's least-celebrated book. I suspect I know why: it is dark and truth-telling in ways that upset today's professional-class sensibilities.

In particular, his emphasis on hard work as the basis of the good society cuts against all digital-age aspirations, in which the goal is to do as little as possible. For me, the book came at exactly the right moment. Disabused of my past techno-utopianism, demoralized by the spectacular failure of ideological systems to resist lockdowns, and shattered by the triangulating schemes of party politics, I realized that I too had lost touch with normal life in all its authenticity, simplicity, and beauty. More than that, the values that undergird such a life, a life of genuine freedom, needed refurbishment and restoration.

Here is my personal attempt to recapture some of what we lost in these years. It is a commentary following Sloane's themes with the addition of some of my own. Some versions of these thoughts previously appeared in the *Epoch Times*, which provides me with the implausible generosity of printing my articles six times per week, and Brownstone Institute, our beloved project to rekindle an honest intellectual culture in times of corruption and censorship.

My appreciation for all my colleagues, friends, and loved ones is incalculable; a list of them all would be impossibly long. My thoughts are a product of my engagements in these years in which our legacy communities were smashed by force. I think of all today who have the strength to write, read, and hope as survivors.

The question this book seeks to answer is why have we the living been blessed with another day and what are we to do with our lives? As we approach the 250th anniversary of America's birth, these are questions that bear careful reflection.

The Meaning of the Semiquincentennial

LOCKE

The word semiquincentennial is not likely to catch on – it's too hard to say – but it means the 250th anniversary. For the USA, that happens July 4, 2026, because we count our birthday from one of the most remarkable documents issued in the history of man: the Declaration of Independence.

That alone is notable. We don't date our birth from the Articles of Confederation, the ratification of the US Constitution, or back much earlier to the landing on Plymouth Rock. No, we date it from the time when some men representing everyone said that we are now independent from the British empire. We can and will govern ourselves.

The nation's birthday is not the government's birthday. It marks instead a revolution against government.

The Americans did not want a war with Britain and they knew that such a declaration would likely provoke a wider one. Like all wars, this one war was a disaster, giving rise to death and inflation and traumatizing the happy life that most people were living at the time. On the other hand, the trauma of war forged a new national identity.

It is called a revolution but it was different from the later French case – or the many in British history – because it was not merely an attempt to replace the current government with a new one, much less start history anew. It is sometimes called a "conservative revolution" because the purpose was restorative. The colonies simply wanted the right to live as they had come to expect, without the ravages and exploitations that came with being subject to the British Crown.

That said, the document was certainly not lacking in ideals. Oddly, these ideals came from the British philosopher John Locke and his *Second Treatise on Government*. Entire sections of this book came to be paraphrased in the Declaration in much more poetic and memorable form.

The Declaration said: "We hold these truths to be self-evident, that all men are created equal, that they are endowed by their Creator with certain unalienable Rights, that among these are Life, Liberty and the pursuit of Happiness. — That to secure these rights, Governments are instituted among Men, deriving their just powers from the consent of the governed, — That whenever any Form of Government becomes destructive of these ends, it is the Right of the People to alter or to abolish it, and to institute new Government, laying its foundation on such principles and organizing its powers in such form, as to them shall seem most likely to effect their Safety and Happiness."

It's hard at this stage of history to recapture the sheer radicalism of the above passage. It sums up the whole of political science and ethics as it pertains to politics. The author Thomas Jefferson replaced Locke's phrase "Life, liberty, and property" with "Life, liberty, and the pursuit of happiness" because of the long confusion over the meaning of property, which, in the British case, was compromised by Royal grants of privilege that the Americans rejected. Here we simply embrace freedom and opportunity, which of course is inclusive of property rights but broader.

Remember that at the time, many Americans held slaves. And yet here was Jefferson proclaiming all men to be equal in rights. For this reason, and it was a very good one, many suspected that Jefferson was a secret abolitionist. He was indeed. Eventual emancipation was already baked into the fabric of what America is all about. It took too long to happen and the horrible war that brought it about should have never taken place but we eventually got there.

My first time traveling outside the US I had a sudden shock – an obvious revelation and one that is probably only surprising to Americans – that we are not the only country in the world and the only culture that is robust, meaningful, and contributes to human flourishing. Any foreign person reading those sentences knows exactly what I mean: Americans really do think this way, and it is embarrassing.

As time has gone on, however, and I've travelled the world many times, I've come to realize just how influential and important America really is to world flourishing. I do not just mean the military empire which breeds much resentment. I mean the ideals as articulated above. Most everyone in the world knows the text. The notion of human rights has animated politics ever since, which is striking to consider since no such thing existed in the ancient world.

I hear often that what happens in America very often foreshadows what happens around the world. This is why so many people today are looking at what is happening in the current renewal taking place. You can agree with everything

Trump is doing or disagree with it all but there is no question in anyone's mind that dramatic changes are taking place.

The main theme of change at the 250th anniversary is the restoration of the American spirit. That includes free speech, transparency in government, rights for the people, limits on the excesses of power, free enterprise in economics, human choice in religion, freedom in education and health care, an end to military empire, and the right to pursue happiness in general.

Hardly anyone alive in any country would disagree that all these ideas need a reboot at the end of these very confusing times. We need to rediscover the foundations of civilized life, and recapture the spirit that made America great.

I was young during the Bicentennial celebrations in 1976. I see now why they were so significant. The upheavals of the previous decade – the burning cities, the assassinations, the draft riots, and finally the impeachment of the president – were finally behind us. There were existing struggles at the time such as gas lines, inflation, and economic stagnation (not to mention bad fashion). All that said, 1976 did certainly become a turning point in US history.

The 250th anniversary can be a turning point too. Perhaps this country is not destined to go the way of so many empires before (Mayan, Aztec, Portuguese, Spanish, Habsburg, British) by ending in bankruptcy, demoralization, and loss of influence. The irony in this case is that the American cultural and ideological empire can only be preserved by reigning in its military and national-security empire. That seems to be the plan, insofar as I understand it.

Will it work? There is some hope that it will. Eventually. Maybe. With many bumps along the way. In any case, we are all enormously fortunate to be alive to watch the unfolding of these events.

The most prescient and hopeful movements in the US now stretch beyond party politics and ideological labels; they center on the restoration of ideals. Just as in 1776, we stand at a precipice. We hope to preserve what is great about this country by rallying around certain principles. Thomas Jefferson took the American experience and framed it into a philosophy, one that has swept the world and remains the dominant orthodoxy of understanding. Our job is simply to recall and make it real again.

Yes, there is every reason to be proud to be an American. But with that must come the humility to recognize that this country can be "more perfect." The pathway there is through a deeper understanding of the Founding, which centered on the rights and powers of the people themselves. That's the theme and the goal, not to create utopia but to re-establish the best-possible framework for people to live their best lives.

The Spirit of Respect

LIFE,
LIBERTY,
AND THE
PURSUIT OF
HAPPINESS

In 1973, as the bicentennial of the US approached, the great American essayist and illustrator Eric Sloane was commissioned to write a book commemorating what is great about America. He focused on what we once had and might be losing.

He chose this theme because he was unique in understanding the American experience of the past. He had already written and illustrated several evocative books on Americana, and his voice came to be beloved in circles centered on literary nostalgia.

The result is a fascinating small volume called *The Spirits of '76*, as published by Walker Press. Long out of print, it makes for enthralling reading. Though I cannot hope to match his insight, it occurred to me to revive his main themes.

All of Sloane's work is worth revisiting. A large collection including his gorgeous illustrations are found in *Eric Sloane's America*. You can also visit his museum in Connecticut.

In the short book he wrote for the Bicentennial, he begins with a reflection on the age of the value of the past.

"Man so often comments: 'If we only knew then what we know now," but few of us consider: 'If we only could know now what they knew then!'"

That's a sentence to commit to memory. It embeds a powerful truth. We have forgotten so much, or never learned, what our ancestors knew from hard experience. We've had it easy, but this has also denied us the wisdom that comes from building something from scratch.

We've inherited a castle and never thought to wonder who laid the stones. The problem gets worse as we age, and as the country ages.

"We seldom see ourselves growing older," he writes. "The slow change is insidious and although we are told that time flies, it is hard to realize that it is we who do the flying while time actually stands still: the past is but a moment ago."

Yes, that gives you a flavor of the power of his prose. It never stops being insightful and provocative. He goes on to apply the insight to the history of the US.

"The truth is that 1776 belongs to 1776. We cannot hope to recapture the old ways easily, partly because we have so destroyed our past but also because we ourselves have become different. The godly, frugal, content, thankful, work-loving man of yesterday has now become the money-oriented, extravagant, discontented, thankless, work-shunning man of today."

So, yes, his book is meant as a wake-up call: see who we were so that we can compare with who we have become, as people but also as a nation, and then get better.

"We charm ourselves into believing that we have a birthday each year: the truth is that there is only one birthday; all the others are merely celebrating that past event. Stopping long enough to glance backward to see where we once were and where we are now can be enlightening, possibly critical."

The first subject he chooses concerns what he calls "the spirit of respect." I tried but failed to anticipate what he means with this word, but it becomes clear quickly. He proposes the word respect as a replacement for the word patriotism, which he finds too much wrapped up in the history of warfare. The Vietnam experience did indeed loom large in those days.

Respect in his view covers the whole of what is good about patriotism but is inclusive of so much more. It means respect for country and the symbolism thereof, including its music, national anthems, and flag. More than that, it is about respect for the inner air of what these symbols mean to signify.

Above all else, they signify freedom. That is for him the essence of the American idea.

With respect for freedom comes respect for that which freedom grants unto us, including faith, family, community, the dignity of oneself, and the dignity of others. He found tremendous evidence of this idea in American history and worried already in 1973 that this attitude was ever more rare.

Of course, he was writing in a time of tremendous crisis in American life. The draft riots, the assassinations, the political scandals, and the loss of cultural identity were fresh on everyone's mind.

Hardly anyone in 1973 was particularly interested in celebrating America's 200th birthday because patriotism had become so demeaned and diminished as a cultural force. It was a time just following the rise of a countercultural movement that aggressively rejected everything having to do with respect for faith, family, and individual dignity.

It occurs to me to be grateful about all that we have regained in these 50 years. Despite everything, the place of freedom and family and community does seem to have made a comeback. The demoralization that the generation of those years seems to have yielded to a new clarity, at least concerning what needs to be done.

In the spirit of updating his text, consider what might be unique about the American respect for country.

Countless times in my travels and conversations with people from abroad, I have heard them say some version of the following: Americans are fortunate to have a history that is defined by love of liberty and rights, and to have these themes codified in your founding documents.

It's an interesting point to consider. Many European and Latin American countries have rich and glorious histories, with ups and downs, revolutions and counterrevolutions, leaders good and bad, times of poverty and times of plenty. Every citizen of Mexico, Portugal, Italy, and Poland feels this and loves their countries' histories, and rightly so, taking pride in many features.

America might actually be distinct in having a definite birthday that coincided with a document that ended up pretty much serving as a global template for what government is, what rights are and to whom they belong, and a long list of examples of what it means for government to do things it should not do.

I speak of the Declaration of Independence. More than any document in the history of politics, its influence has been felt the world over and continues to rise to this day.

I'm not sure any country in the world can boast such a thing. It has certainly left a mark on what America aspires to be. We even fought a civil war to make sure that ideals were achieved, and later attempted to perfect those ideas with the civil rights movement.

Despite all the various interpretations and fights over how to get there, this document does serve as a kind of shared understanding of civic life.

The author of the Declaration was Thomas Jefferson, who took the main ideas therein from his study of John Locke and the French liberal tradition. He refined those ideas and wrote a small treatise for the ages. For many of the men who signed it, it was a death warrant and they knew that when they put their signatures on that parchment. Their sacrifices gave birth to a new order for the ages.

A few years ago, I revisited Monticello, the home that Jefferson built. I took the tour, which had been revised to fit in with 2010s-era fashion for hating on the Founding Fathers. The guide had almost nothing good to say about Jefferson, who, despite failings, has long been revered the world over as a voice of emancipation.

This "woke" tour broke my heart. The first chapter of this book by Sloane makes this point. The tour simply denied Jefferson the respect he deserves. The experience thereby denied the Declaration and the America to which it gave birth the respect they deserve. I do hope this tour changes soon. I suspect it will, if it hasn't already.

To say that America was born at a distinct time in history is not to disparage the Colonial experience or the long history of the natives of this continent. Indeed, America has always revered both, from its adoration of the Plymouth legends to its long celebration of the American Indian in its iconography and coinage.

When Senator Elizabeth Warren claimed Native ancestry, she might not have been deliberately lying. Many generations of people from her class and region wrongly believed they had native ancestry, and claimed it as a matter not of victimhood but pride. It's just a funny tick of New England culture, adding some perception of rootedness and perspicacity we have long associated with such a background. That it turned out to be false was genuinely a surprise to her.

Because of this birthday, which is not in dispute despite some attempts to change that, and the document with which it is associated, American civic culture is marked by ideals in ways most people in the world have only histories. This is not to put down others, but only to say that Americans are deeply fortunate to have this and claim it.

This is what Sloane was getting at with his idea of respect. To have it requires knowledge, pride, and a certain appreciation approaching piety. You surely feel it when you hear "God bless America." The song represents a wish, hope, and prayer, one rooted in respect for our country's ideals above all else.

The Spirit of Work

"I'm not straightening ties for $4.50 an hour."

Those immortal words are still with me. They were uttered to me in private when I worked at a men's store when I was 17. It was from a coworker. The boss had just walked by and suggested that so long as there were no customers in the store, we should get busy making the products more wonderful.

My co-worker balked at the idea. It got me thinking. The store was not paying him to stand around. They were paying him to put value in order to get value out. They also have to pay the bills otherwise, which means that arguably an employee needs to add far MORE value into the company than he takes out.

The employment contract doesn't work like a vending machine. You don't stick money in and get a snack out. Employers invest in their employees, paying them far more than they are worth in the training period in hopes of subsidizing the losses on the other side. This is why anyone on the clock should be thrilled for the opportunity to work harder, become more valuable, and give back to his benefactors.

My friend did not get this. Sure enough, he was fired a few weeks later. As it should be. That kid wanted a "work/life balance." He got it but without the remunerative work. By the way, I despise that half-century-old phrase. It implies that work is not part of life, and that a good life consists mainly of sloth. What an awful ethic!

The second chapter of Eric Sloane's wonderful *The Spirits of '76*, as published in 1973, covers the topic of work beautifully.

He says that hard work is a great American virtue that has seen much better days.

His chapter is mostly about finding love in one's work, doing it not for the money (which is a sign, a symbol, a necessity) but because you adore making value with your hands and your mind. You will never really end up doing anything truly wonderful based on a financial incentive alone. Nor does competition – beating the other guy – suffice. Great achievements are born from within, a result of a dream, a dedication, a true love of making your life worth something.

I adore this chapter because all of this is completely forgotten. It's much worse today than it was in the 1970s. For two and a half decades, the Fed has mostly been running a system of zero interest rates, which has ballooned up the corporate and financial sectors to appalling levels. For decades now, hiring has not really been about value in and value out, but the purchase of warm bodies with credentials.

Several generations now have been raised without remunerative labor in their teens, so they graduate from colleges with one, two, or three degrees without having the slightest knowledge of or experience with actual work. During all their prime years, from 16 to 25, they have learned all the wrong habits: sleep late, stay out late, do the minimum to get by, party like crazy, always put sloth above focus, friends above obligation, and comfort above anything that would result in stress, toil, or pain.

You can't build productive economies this way. You can't

build happy lives this way. Even worse, you end up with a caste system: the well-to-do who live on the Internet versus everyone else.

With that has come a routine judgment of others based on their job and status: the less you have to work and the higher your pay, the greater the status. The more you have to work for every dime, the lower your status. Some people will simply not do a "low" job because they imagine themselves better.

This is not the attitude of a free society; it is the bias of a caste system. It breeds not community but disdain.

Something has to change. It likely will. It already is. Firings in general are on the rise in every sector. People assume that is a terrible thing. Actually, it could be the best thing that ever happened to people.

Here's a story of a young woman I hired once and fired for incompetence. I was amazed that she later put me down as a reference for a future employee. That man called me. Thinking this through carefully, I said two things.

First, she was an awful employee. She did not complete her tasks. She complained constantly. She prioritized her social media over her job. She was unreliable. We were better off the instant she left the company.

The man on the phone said that this was the worst reference he had ever heard. But I told him to hold on.

In my experience, I said, people need to be fired from one or two jobs before they figure it out. They have time to reflect on what went wrong. They never want to have it happen again because the feeling of failure and financial insecurity is so profoundly depressing.

I continued: "Something tells me that she could now be a wonderful employee. That she put me down as a reference tells you something. She is confident that she knows and I know what went wrong. It suggests that she is ready for a change. I say hire her. She could be your best worker ever."

He thanked me for the strangest work reference conversation he had ever had. He called back a year later. You know the final chapter of this story: he said that she was indeed fantastic. She had apparently learned something from the experience of having been fired. She is the most earnest and hard-working employee ever. You are welcome, I said.

If you have teenage kids, you know how extremely difficult it is to get them a job anyway, but a job is exactly what they need. They need another source of influence and authority in their lives outside school and home. They need to mix in an adult world, to have an example to which to aspire. They need to encounter complaining customers, grueling hours, exhaustion, difficult coworkers, and impatient bosses.

This is called: adventure! It is far more exciting than being chained to a desk 8 hours a day, 5 days a week, and learning to live for weekend fripperies. Sadly since 1936, there have been severe legal restrictions on teenage work. You cannot really have a full-time job until you are 18.

It's no wonder the labor force participation rate for 16-19-year-olds has gone from 60 percent to 35 percent. It's sad. It means losing the one chance in life you have to develop a genuine work ethic as a daily habit.

These days, we habitually treat work as regrettable and only leisure as desirable. This is absurd. The message is only reinforced by the invention of this idea of "retirement," which is another 1930s artifact. In real life, everyone should be thrilled with the opportunity to dispense of idleness and become useful for something, whether you are paid for it or not.

In fact, and this does take us far afield, I would like to see the rise of old-style unpaid apprenticeships or maybe even work arrangements for work in which the worker actually pays in order to gain experience. All of this is technically and pointlessly illegal now.

Someone in the Trump administration recommended recently that all taxes should be removed for young workers. That's a fantastic idea. Something has to break this crazy mentality of lazy entitlement that has seized so many. You cannot build a country like this or even have a good life.

Happy workers are happy people – regardless of what you do. We are all born into this world to make ourselves useful, not merely to kvetch about having our streaming services interrupted by a demand that we achieve something.

Hard work is a virtue. There is no line between work and life; they are the same. We used to know that. That's how this country was built: with blood, sweat, tears, and heavy tools and long hours. To be inert is to be miserable.

We can find our way back to the work ethic, but it is going

to require not just changes in what we do but how we think. It might even require straightening ties for $4.50 an hour.

The Spirit of Frugality

Did you ever hang out at the local dump and rummage through the stuff? I certainly did. My father took me there all the time. He loved digging through things and marveling at what people throw away. I swear he saw this trash as treasure. We never took any home, but he always explained his thinking at every step.

I never told my friends about this because I thought it was too weird. My father was actually a historian of the old school. He loved a good story with evidence to back it. He found millions of them in the city dump. That's why we went. It wasn't research as such; it was just a passion, a deep curiosity about what others found to be worthless enough to throw out.

He was looking for the opposite: evidence that people have no clue what is valuable and what is not. Too often people simply do not know, which is why so many thrift stores are packed with treasures. I could go from one thrift store to another all day, all weekend, every week. They thrill me to the same extent they disgust others.

America specializes in making trash and throwing things away. We see that as a symbol of how prosperous we are. Our ancestors did not think this way. They saw prosperity as linked with how much they could save and how little they spent unnecessarily.

Economics teaches that savings requires deferred consumption. That means thinking about the future more than the present. Savings is also the foundation of investment. Investment is the basis of prosperity. Add it all up and you get this: sacrificing the comforts of today is the key to a better tomorrow.

Hardly anyone would argue with the above. It is stated very plainly in ways that make it entirely logical and unobjectionable.

And yet let's add in one word: macroeconomics, especially as interpreted by John Maynard Keynes. He posited such a thing as the "paradox of thrift." This happens when people save too much and don't spend. Aggregate demand goes down and crushes producer hopes.

Business dries up, so we fall into depression, in Keynes's view, which requires the central bank to print money and Congress to spend even to the point of national indebtedness. That's the real key to prosperity, said Keynes: running up big debts and printing your way out. Also, government should take over investment.

I'm not going to explain the above further because it is wholly wrong. It is entirely based on fallacies punctuated by complicated language. That was Keynes's specialty. He somehow managed to bamboozle generations of academics and lawmakers into setting their common sense on the shelf.

A casualty of Keynesianism was the gradual deprecation of frugality in American culture. This is the theme of the third chapter of Eric Sloane's book. He too begins with reflections on thrift stores as symbols of frugality and its abandonment.

Quite often, he says, people will be in these stores and yell at the high prices.

"My father had one of those and threw it away. Why should this be so expensive?"

This misses the point entirely. It is precisely because his father threw that away that the surviving ones that are obtainable catch such a high price. Our ancestors worked much harder to keep what was valuable and threw away only what was useless or simply had to go. They tried never to acquire what they did not need.

Of course they did without, sometimes by necessity but also because they believed it was right.

My grandmother had a huge stack of quilts that I loved, but they were strange. They seemed all to be made of scraps of things. I asked her once. She said that her mother had sewn them from the tattered dresses worn by her 10 sisters. After hand-me-downs had run their course, they became blankets.

I kept one until it literally fell apart. I always treasured that blanket as embedding deep history but also a profound ethic of frugality.

Several generations have gone by since we met any really frugal person. I mean people who simply would never go out to eat, paying four times what it would cost to make at home, people who would never buy retail when it can be picked up at a Goodwill and so on. I'm a bit that way, but mostly performatively: I shop all the time on eBay and various online marketplaces with used things.

But it's not the same. We don't much care about waste anymore. We really should. With waste comes a lack of appreciation for the sacrifices others have made to bring us material blessings. And once you focus on frugality, it can be fun. See how far you can stretch things. Never empty unused groceries into the bin; figure out dishes to make to use them before they go bad. Learn to stitch your clothes rather than toss them. Look through your credit card statements to eliminate all subscriptions you don't use.

And so on.

What is the point? Here is the paradox. The point is to become prosperous. We live poor in order to be rich. This is truly the difference between old and new money. It comes down to the frugality of the old money.

I once knew an extremely wealthy man who paid to put marble floors in his front entrance but balked at paying to paint the closets because no one would ever see them. Granted, he was a bit crazy, but he had a spirit of frugality even if it appeared in strange ways.

Our ancestors canned food. They froze leftovers. They handed down clothes. They made rags out of old sheets. They knew how to sew, bake, clean, paint, sand, saw, and so much more. We know none of this and it is sad. Today we think everything is at the store, waiting for us, and we toss anything and everything that becomes even slightly out of fashion. It's all ridiculous.

And look at household debt! It's awful. And the country's debt: it is worse, even unpayable. We've paid a heavy price for behaving this way.

It's easy to start with frugality. Stop buying things you don't need, especially silly products like cleaning supplies when vinegar, bleach, baking soda, and other basics work as well or better. And here is one to which you will object and fine: I'm down on toothpaste which is sticky and sweet and mostly a racket. Plain baking soda costs a fraction as much and does a much better job.

I'm not going to offer any more in this list except to say that frugality is not a set of instructions; it is a mindset of buying only what you need, saving what is valuable, and throwing out only what is useless. It's sport and delightful.

The way things are headed economically right now, I suspect more of us are going to adopt frugality sooner rather than later. We might even find ourselves rummaging through the city dump to find treasures that others have mistakenly thrown out.

The Spirit of Thankfulness

HOLY
BIBLE

It's no longer fashionable to pray before meals, especially with guests around. Don't want to offend anyone, invoke a god someone else rejects, or otherwise be seen as old-fashioned or superstitious. I get it, and I too feel the sense that we should all just sit down and start eating.

But you know what? No matter how long the habit of not praying before meals has been with us – is it decades or a half-century or more? – it always seems like something is missing. Something is supposed to happen that does not happen. When we start eating, I cannot shake the sense that we are not supposed to be doing that.

Maybe it is because I was raised in a very religious home, and Dad always used the family prayer before meals to either make a point to the kids or train them in how to practice piety and gratitude.

Yes, that is it: thankfulness. This is the theme of the fourth chapter of Eric Sloane's 1973 book on the Bicentennial, a mini-treatise on what America was and could be again. His theme concerning thankfulness reflects a bit on the holiday of Thanksgiving.

It long predates the founding. It started in 1621 as a copy of the Indian tradition. It took place in June. It gradually moved from the time of George Washington all the way to FDR when it finally landed as the fourth Thursday of November.

It is intriguing that it ranks among the top favorite American holidays, has no precedent in the religious calendar, and doesn't seem to be practiced in other countries. Sloane believes that

America had a unique appreciation of thankfulness because we built the country from a native land into the greatest country on earth, all the while never leaving our historical roots.

Maybe that is right. Regardless, he is also correct to say in 1973 that the attitude of gratitude toward our blessings seemed to be dying. We stopped at some point even imagining our lives without material plenty and thereby took it all for granted, thus no longer giving thanks. Why give thanks for that to which one is entitled?

It's true that Thanksgiving has become rather humdrum as compared with when I was a kid. It was a big deal back then because we rarely had big meals. We had small meals and never went out to eat. It was mostly the same thing over and over, not because my parents were poor but rather because they learned frugality from their parents.

So when the whole family would gather around a huge turkey, vast rolls and veggies, and pies everywhere, it was quite a sight and a feast. Now one wonders why we bother except as performance art. We eat great food daily and have huge meals all the time. We order from menus with 30 choices and get what we want. The stores are filled with endless choice.

Where is the distinct experience of this one meal? For our ancestors, Thanksgiving was preceded by a long period of fasting. That does not mean not eating. It means eating plain food, less food, not much food, staying trim and fit, denying ourselves, and otherwise working hard. The meal of Thanksgiving was a symbol of plenty for which people thanked God and his blessings.

The mealtime prayer was an acknowledgement that we deserve nothing – nature is barren and dangerous – and yet blessings have been bestowed upon us. Food is only one of them. It is for nourishment. But there are so many more. We dare not devour it without considering the possibility of its absence. So too with all our material possessions.

Praying is also a way of saying that our blessings will not change us into spoiled and entitled children but rather remind us of to whom we owe real thanks. It is an act of humility. It brings people together. And like a good toast at cocktail hour, a prayer for meals becomes a community activity, something memorable that people can share as one.

Just practically speaking, it signals: time to eat. If nothing else, that serves a genuine function in every gathering.

How do we get around the problem of interfaith gatherings? My suggestion is don't be shy about your faith tradition. State it up front and then pray in that tradition. All decent people will appreciate it. If you are shy, you can adopt a thing I do, which is pray in Latin so that no one understands it anyway.

Another shift that seems to be taking place in American life is a turn toward healthiness, and that has meant new interest in fasting. Great. We all need this for mind and body. I've taken to doing periodic three-day fasts of coffee in the morning (not giving that up) and water otherwise. But many people have had success with OMAD or One Meal A Day.

A friend of mine has lost a quick 25 pounds doing OMAD

three times per week, without using any of those crazy weight-loss drugs.

There are also new practices of Dry January and so on taking hold. All to the good. Anything to remind us of what it means to do without, so that we can be more thankful for what we have.

It was only several generations ago that all Catholics practiced strict Lent: no meat at all except on Sundays and only one normal meal and two smaller meals that together do not equal one meal. All that went by the wayside in the late sixties, and robbed Catholics of a distinct cultural identity (they were once disparaged as Mackerel Snappers).

This is a sad loss culturally, as is the loss of thankfulness in general. But all of us can make a change in our own lives. We can make up a prayer before meals, even if it is to no one deity in particular but just forces beyond our control. We can learn to fast. We can learn to feel gratitude for our blessing, which we all can find if we look hard enough.

America still has a major holiday devoted to Thanksgiving, but it is also something our heritage celebrates every day. Granted, it is hard to be thankful for that to which you feel entitled. We can all work on that, remembering that by nature and by right we are owed nothing. All that comes to us is a manifestation of some level of beneficence of some kind, whether from God, family, coworkers, community, or just people who make the world work for us.

One of the nicest traditions is the American commercial habit of saying mutual thank-yous. When you get your groceries, you say thank you. They say thank you back. This is because you have both given each other a gift of your own free will. It could be otherwise. We want to make sure it will always be so by letting others know of our gratitude.

America is a commercial culture, but we have always managed to recognize that this means it is also a gift-giving culture, each of us bringing what we have to others to improve their lot and our own at the same time. Let us be thankful to live in such a country, and work to recall and recover the tradition of Thanksgiving that made it so.

The Spirit of Pioneering

JOURNEY

Of all the chapters in Eric Sloane's book, his fifth chapter on pioneering is the most melancholy. He reflects on the hardships of life in the 18th and 19th centuries, the strange and spectacular ways people unrooted themselves to travel for months on end to find new homes in uncharted land and make new homes for themselves, leaving all comforts behind.

They had adventure, but we do not, certainly not in our push-button, app-driven lives of endless electronics, software, and now AI, which tells us everything to think so that we don't have to. We see adventure on screens but don't participate in it. We watch it but don't create it. We admire it from afar but work hard to keep it at bay so that it never really touches us.

I often think about my great-great-great-grandfather, son of a Massachusetts Congregationalist minister, who at the age of 18 in 1830 happened upon a flyer advertising freedom and adventure in Texas. For whatever reason, he left. I don't know why. It seems crazy because he had every privilege. He seemed to want something else, perhaps to make it on his own.

He made a stop in New Orleans and met with an uncle who gave him tools, horses, and a covered wagon, which he took to East Texas and started farming. He didn't like it and sold it all and made it to Southwest Texas to learn blacksmithing as an apprentice. He later set up his own shop.

He participated in the war for independence from Mexico and then enjoyed a brief period as a Texas Ranger in the Republic before it became a state. Having married, he had a son who found himself embroiled in the Civil War, not fighting

Yankees but going West to settle more lands. He was a medic because he had tools, not because he had medical skills.

Strange times.

No need to tell the whole story, which is quite dramatic, but if you have ever been to the Big Bend, you know the terrain. There seems to be no water. It is scary and threatening. It is hot, dusty, and dry, seemingly gentle on the beautiful surface but angry just beneath. Why did he not just turn around and go home?

It's hard to say, but this much is clear: that generation was made of sterner stuff. And there were many thousands just like him, spreading out from New England in all directions. They cleared land. They planted crops. They figured out the water situation. They felled trees and built homes. They started businesses. They struggled daily to survive and work their way toward the ability to thrive.

That experience is still visible in our culture, but the rationale is gone.

Do you know the wonderful books *Little House on the Prairie*? I hope so. They tell the story but don't neglect *Farmer Boy* and the books by the author's daughter, Rose Wilder Lane. What a writer and what a visionary!

The subject matter should be understood by every American kid and owned by every American family. Our pioneer history shaped this country and its love of freedom and its passion for the new and the possible.

We are no longer pioneers. You could say that we still invent things. We still start businesses and embark on innovations. But we do not venture into wholly unchartered territory and plant our own flag to make a new life for ourselves.

Elon Musk tries to revive all this with his talk about colonizing Mars. I admit that this just does not inspire me. First, it is not going to happen. Second, why would we want it to happen? Third, this just sounds like a big lame excuse for abandoning the job we have to do right here. It seems odd to me to say "Make America Great Again," but if we fail, we can all move to Mars.

Just a few choice quotes from Sloane on this whole subject.

"Adventure is not outside a man, but within."

"Without adventure, civilization is automatically in the process of decay."

"Each scientific advance makes life simpler but duller, without adventure."

There is truth in all this, and this chapter ends without a solution. Perhaps that is how it must be. In the end, if we are to be pioneers again, we have to figure it out one life at a time.

The French word entrepreneurship captures a way to achieve this in the commercial sphere. It means to start something new, take responsibility for the product and accounting and hiring. It is the hardest job you will ever have. Most people fail, of course, and you might as well.

Why do Americans keep starting businesses then? I've always thought about that. After 2020, when so many were closed by force, I wondered if there would ever be another new business in this country again. And yet, once the crisis was over, they popped up again, and people gladly forgot about what happened.

That's amazing. It's like Americans refuse to be demoralized. We keep believing no matter what. We want to have good lives, and we believe that this is the country to do it in. That's the spirit of pioneering. It is not lost. It has just ebbed and flowed.

When Sloane was writing in 1973, there must have been a feeling of despair in the culture. The economy was awful. Politics was corrupt. Cities had been wrecked. There was this generation gap that tore apart families. I'm not sure things seemed hopeful.

And yet the Bicentennial came and went and life got better. Then worse. Then better. And so on. But it seems like no depths have ever really defeated this country. Even in the darkest days of lockdown and all that followed, the spirit was still there. The spirit of adventure, the romance of the pioneer, is still within us.

It can be fully unleashed again. One hopes that is where we are headed again. In which case, we can be newly inspired by our past as a culture and a country. From sea to shining sea, this country was built in a very short time by human hands inspired by the desire to be great at whatever the cost.

The music still rings out in our imaginations and can again in our lives.

The Spirit of Godliness

HOLY
BIBLE

In my youth, we sang a hymn that went: "You ask me how I know he lives; he lives within my heart."

Honestly, I'm not sure that this line made much sense to me as a kid, at least not to an aspirational rationalist. As years have gone by, I have a better understanding. It's a distinctly American idea.

It seems to be pointing to the truth that faith is ultimately a personal matter, the most personal matter. It is something we accept or reject as a matter of the life of the individual mind and heart. That is how we know.

That is the very essence of the American experience with religion, which is the subject of the sixth chapter of Eric Sloane's book. This chapter is on "godliness."

Regardless of the belief structure, faith tradition, or denominational affiliation, the American experience has required that every religion draw its adherents based on personal choice. You can accept or reject.

Maybe that doesn't sound radical today, but there was a time when such a system was outlandish and seemingly unworkable. Around the time that the colonists arrived at Plymouth, the religious wars were still raging in Europe, as fallout from the Reformation. The perception was that every country had to choose: Protestant or Catholic. You could not have freedom of choice.

Why was this? Because church and state had been long tied together. The church signed off on the political leadership, and the political leadership gave protection to the church. They had made a deal that lasted a millennium. When the Reformation took place, chaos broke out. People fought it out.

In time, of course, and about the same period that American colonial life was emerging as a rich and good experience, the religious wars gradually came to an end. They were expensive in lives and property. The notion of liberty in the modern sense was born and germinated over time.

As it turns out, everyone is better off simply deciding for themselves and their families what faith to follow. All this system asks is that we tolerate the decisions of others as they tolerate ours. There is peace at last.

The colonies at first attempted official religions with a European-style mix of church and state, but it never really took hold. People were moving around too much. Many were only in America because they were religious dissidents. They had a history of being put upon. Why would they do that to others? They were grateful enough for the freedom to believe and practice.

Plus, there were better things to do than fight over faith. They had houses to build, towns to found, civic matters to tend to, and the crops and livestock always needed attention.

The Americans were simply too busy to bother with religious wars. By the time of the founding, it seemed pretty obvious what the new system should be. There should be absolute freedom of religion. It was put in the First Amendment to the US Constitution.

"Congress shall make no law respecting an establishment

of religion, or prohibiting the free exercise thereof."

Amazing words! The whole of recorded history was a story about people killing and dying and pillaging over religious struggles. The Americans had this crazy idea: let people believe what they want to believe just so long as they let others do the same.

This did not harm religious practice. Quite the opposite. Films recreating the Colonial and Founding experience don't show this, but faith was everywhere present in people's lives. Religion was the basis of education, civic celebrations, health care and hospitals, care for widows and orphans, and so much more.

Faith was life and life was faith. Both were woven together by this idea called freedom.

It began to catch on around the world, while the Americans began to embrace it even more. In the 19th century, there were waves of religious revivalism leading to every manner of belief structure and religious leader. America became the home for what might be called religious entrepreneurship. Someone would experience a calling and set up a religion and recruit members.

Something like this would have been unthinkable in the old world. In the new, it seemed possible. That is how this country became the home to so many diverse faiths. It's astonishing to consider how many. Nothing shocks us really. We are temperamentally happy for people to believe whatever they want so long as they do the same for others.

We look back at wars fought between the believers in transubstantiation and consubstantiation, complete with stockades and hangings, and we simply cannot imagine such a thing. Yes, some historic faiths took a while to come around to this idea of religious freedom, but even the Catholic Church came around to the notion by 1963.

For the most part, and despite well-known exceptions in our history, the idea of religious freedom has been an integral part of the American experience. This is what made it so shocking and appalling that in 2020-21, many churches were forcibly closed and religious observance restricted based on claims of public health.

I knew at the time that this would be a bridge too far. Mess with people's faith and you create a lifetime of fury. For example, the legacy media was raging against Jewish weddings and funerals that ignored "social distancing." Sorry, but some matters are more important than the public-health schemes of government officials.

I seriously doubt that anything like this will happen again in our lifetimes. Ironically, it has led to a huge revival of faith in America. The houses of worship are filling up again. Belief is on the rise after decades of advancing secularism. In other words, some bad actors tried to stamp it out but ended up causing a wave of religious revivalism – again!

This is the American story. We tried a new experiment in letting all flowers bloom. It created the greatest garden of diverse faith the world has ever seen. It stands now as an example to everyone. This is another American gift to the world. The freedom of conscience owes so much to the history of this nation.

The Spirit of Agronomy

It's impossible to speak of American history without reference to the life of the farmer and the land. The experience shaped many generations. It formed the basis for the belief in freedom itself, the conviction that a family can provide for itself through hard work and defend its rights based on the little slice of physical land that the family controlled.

Read any of the writings of the Founding Fathers, and you find an unrelenting romanticization of life on the land. ""When I first entered on the stage of public life," wrote Thomas Jefferson, "I came to a resolution never . . . to wear any other character than that of a farmer."

The idea rattles us a bit. We don't really have agronomy anymore. We live in cities, type on laptops, play with digits, farm information, and our only connection with food is the grocery store and restaurant.

Reading Jefferson, then, makes one think: we don't live on farms anymore, so all must be lost. That, of course, is untrue. His point is simply that the agrarian life provides a bulwark, not that you cannot have freedom if it gives way to other modes of living.

And the agrarian life did give way, for reasons both organically evolving but also through force, which is deeply regrettable. As the Industrial Revolution advanced, fewer and fewer people lived on farms. We moved to the cities. By 1920, it was pretty well done: industry beat agriculture in its overall contribution to American productivity.

For most of my adult life, I made fun of people who had

regrets about this. What's wrong with corporate farming? It's feeding the world and we would starve otherwise. We need big companies, huge machinery, oceans of pesticide and fertilizer, and consolidated supply chains. We simply cannot and should not go back.

I've come to change my mind, however, now that I've been so heavily exposed to a critique of industrial food and Big Agriculture. I see now that it is not entirely natural and normal that they would have replaced small farms.

Last year, I drove to the countryside, pulled over at a farmers' market, and had a long conversation with the husband and wife who ran the farm and the meat and vegetable stand. They talked of their struggles with the weather, of course, and dealing with the exigencies of nature.

Mostly, they spoke of the artificial struggles they face. They are hit relentlessly with tax on land, taxes on production, taxes on profits, taxes on everything. There are regulations too. They are prevented from selling directly to stores. They face grueling restrictions on meat processing. The health inspectors drive them nuts. They face constraints on wages, hourly restrictions on labor, and wrangle with bureaucrats constantly.

Without all of this, they are certain that they could make a better go of it. They could compete with the big guys. After all, their products are healthier, more delicious, and just overall better. No question, they said, that they could compete and win on a fair playing field. As it stands, they barely survive.

I've come to appreciate that point of view. Imagine if we

suddenly did have a free market in agriculture. No taxes, no regulations, no mandates, no restrictions. Anyone can raise food, process it, and sell it to whomever under any conditions. In other words, what if today we had the same system we had in the time of Jefferson and Washington?

We would see an absolute explosion in small farms. Everyone would be selling eggs. Produce would be everywhere and so would meat. We would learn not to depend on grocery stores and supercenters but our friends and neighbors. The idea of eating locally would not have to be preached by anyone; it would just become our daily routine again.

This is because everyone prefers local produce over industrially shipped and packaged corporate food. We only have the ubiquity of the latter due to subsidies, taxes, and other restrictions and interventions.

Could we still feed the world? It might be the wrong question. The real question is: Can the world feed itself? The answer is yes. How do we know? Because the human experience is a very long one, and we have the evidence. So long as governments leave people alone, humanity does indeed figure out a way to feed itself.

Maybe that point seems obvious when stated that way. But it was not so obvious to me when I thought we needed mega-corporations and every manner of potions and government plans to make it happen. Once I realized that I had believed a lie, I could never go back. Now, I'm all in with the movements that push regenerative farming, condemn chemicals in food, and eschew processed food, which is likely poisoning us all.

When you travel to foreign countries where the agricultural life is still relatively localized – I include fishing in this category – we find much healthier food and better habits of eating overall. We also find healthier people. I'm speaking of Japan, South Korea, Portugal, Chile, and European countries too.

I'm not alone in observing that when I travel to Israel or Spain or Brazil, I can eat like a horse and not gain weight. Why is this? Many people have reported the same.

There is clearly something wrong with the American food supply. I have immigrant friends – Vietnamese, Pakistani, Greek – who simply will not eat American food. They don't trust it. They set up and shop in their own stores with imported products and products made by their own chefs and butchers and farmers they know. Their customers depend on them. They are healthier people overall than the typical American mall dweller.

Something has to change. It could and may. We could deregulate, stop taxing the heck out of farmers, open up markets, make raising local produce and meat easier, or at least stop punishing it. If we took these simple steps, we might indeed see the flourishing of small farmers again.

Why should we not bring the innovative spirit we use in technology to the world of food production too? We simply do not. Instead, all government systems of agriculture pretend as if we found the right answers in the early 1970s and will never change. Actually, much needs to change. We don't need to subsidize grains forever and stick the surplus in everything we eat. We can embrace healthier alternatives.

Thomas Jefferson said: "Cultivators of the earth are the most valuable citizens. They are the most vigorous, the most independent, the most virtuous, and they are tied to their country and wedded to its liberty and interests by the most lasting bonds."

I used to dismiss such thoughts. No more. Maybe he was right. Nor am I willing to give up on agronomy as the foundation of the American way of life. Maybe it can make a return, if only governments would get out of the way.

The Spirit of Time

Sloane's eighth chapter begins with an interesting observation. He was an expert on old-style covered wooden bridges. Strange passion but stick with me here.

He observed that there were always signs on these bridges: "Walk your horse." Apparently galloping across a bridge creates a rhythmic pattern that weakens the structural foundations. To make the bridge secure for longer, people on horses dismounted and walked slowly and deliberately.

He uses this to illustrate a fascinating point about the American perceptions of time in the past. It was really never about haste. The idea of a "New York minute" is new. The old way is patience, discipline, slow achievement, and unrelenting and constant work in all hours.

Sloane points out that if you ever visited an older farmer and see how he works, he is rather slow about it all but never stops going. He does this and does that but never seems to be in a rush. He seeks to do a thorough job, not a quick one. He doesn't get frustrated with the wood that doesn't fit, the nail that is rusted, or the door jam that is off; instead, he just calmly takes it on as another thing to do.

I vaguely recall this as a young man when I worked with my uncle on a roofing job. We climbed up carefully and slowly and started pulling shingles one by one, fixing or replacing them, and moving on to the next one. I quickly grew impatient as I saw the huge length we had to cover. I started to rush my portion and brag about it. He looked at me knowingly.

We worked for hours in the hot sun. Finally, at nearly the noon hour, he said we should take a break. I was deeply grateful, climbed down the ladder, and headed for the water hose. I drank as much and as fast as I could. He muttered a warning about that. Sure enough, I threw up. Blech. He laughed and we went inside.

He sat down and his wife bought him not a gigantic glass of water but a cup of coffee. I sat there gobsmacked. How in the world could he have coffee after 4 hours in the hot sun with nonstop work? Years later, I was still thinking about this.

Sloane has the answer. He didn't work fast or furiously to exhaustion. He worked slowly and deliberately, consistent with his job and his health. He knew what he was doing. I did not.

After the break and a sandwich, we climbed back up. I was intimidated by how much more there was to do. We got back at it. Another three hours went by, and we took another break. We got back up and worked more.

Sure enough, by 5 o'clock on the hour, we finished. I was thrilled and I simply could not believe how two people working steadily and deliberately could have done all that in one day. I felt great pride and still celebrate to this day.

For my uncle it was just another day, which he repeated every day on everything on which he worked.

Sloane says that this is the true American spirit. Not speed. Not haste. Not a quick win. Instead, the sense of time in our history is relentlessness, patience, deliberate, determined, steady, disciplined. Routine not dopamine. This is the foundation of the American sense of time that we have clearly lost.

Speed these days comes at the highest premium. We expect everything to happen fast. We don't read; we watch the movie. We listen to video interviews at twice the pace of the real thing. We generate the AI summary rather than spend an hour reading. We glom onto any technology that turns days into hours and hours into minutes and minutes into seconds.

This distorted sense of time plays into things like business planning. We are supposed to have 5-year plans and 1-year plans for everything. This is supposed to inspire us to build quickly, act fast, stay driven to achieve, and keep us undiverted. I've always been suspicious of this way of thinking.

As I turn this over in my mind, I've always believed that the only real path to long-term success is simply to do a good day's work. Nothing more. Make sure you get from here to there successfully in one day. Do that every day.

In six months or a year, you can look back and say: Wow, look what we have achieved! But there is no point in planning it out. All you can really do is the job one day at a time, solving puzzles and problems as they come.

We've become so obsessed with speed that we are frustrating ourselves that we cannot do it. Instead of loving what we do, and doing it completely and with excellence, our culture trains us to hate what we are doing and only love the thing we are not doing, and rush to do that instead. And we treat the new thing the same as old: a regrettable task.

For that reason, we are always discontent and never fully engaged in the task at hand. We are fidgety and fill ourselves with resentment. Instead, we should learn to love what we must do and do it with patience and completeness so that we can always say: a job well done.

Almost all young people today believe they are afflicted with Attention Deficit Hyperactivity Disorder or ADHD. This supposed disease is entirely made up, never discovered. It is simply a description of people who are in a wild rush and unable to be patient in their studies or work.

Even worse, we have manufactured drugs to fix this supposed affliction. They have a lot in common with street narcotics, but they are acceptable because doctors prescribe them. They cause people to be wildly focused on one thing and do seemingly impossible work, generating weeks of productivity in one all-nighter.

Magic, right? Not so much. I've worked with many people on these drugs. They do amazing things, just not quite the right things. Ask them to revise what they did, and they report barely remembering having done it at all.

After much experience, I concluded that I would rather work with moderately talented people with a predictable, deliberate, and even slow pace of gradual achievement, rather than someone who lives with wild bursts of amazingness that comes and goes and can never be tweaked because it was done in a mental haze. Such people think they are achievers, but actually they just drive everyone else nuts.

I love work, but I've also come to appreciate how crucial it is to mix one's desire to achieve with a passion for doing what one does with precision and completeness, regardless of how long it takes. Thanks to technology and our worship of progress, we have subsidized speed at the expense of quality, rationality, durability, and longevity.

Think where that has landed us. We buy things all the time now – phones, tablets, laptops, electric kitchen gizmos, choppers, and tiny machines of all sorts – that we know for sure are not going to last more than a few years at most.

They will be replaced with more spending and more stuff. We know this, and we do it anyway and yet why? Because we assume that this gadgeting will help us achieve our aims faster.

It's all rather exhausting and mostly wrong. Just look around your kitchen, for example. That juicer machine takes up lots of counter space when a hand-held and operated squeezer fits in a drawer. How much time do you really save? And isn't there some joy you can find in doing things by hand?

Or how about lights and music? Must they all be operated by your phone? What exactly is the downside of standing up and changing the music or turning the light on or off? Truly, this is getting ridiculous. The goal of life is not to lounge on the sofa while pushing buttons to make things happen all around you. Maybe there is some sense of achievement that comes from actually doing something yourself.

Time in America past: slow, deliberate, thorough, and relentless. Time in America present: rushed, haphazard, panicked, sloppy, and with no longevity. It's all just crazy. We live long lives, God willing. We can make the best of them by putting quality over speed, discipline over performance, routine over dopamine, and completeness over the cosmetics of artificial productivity.

In short, we need to get better at hopping off the horse, walking it across the bridge, and helping to make sure the structure lasts for the next person. The sign to which Sloane pointed was correct, and it applies to much more than just old-fashioned covered bridges.

The Spirit of Independence

The word independence is everywhere in American life, even to the point of overuse. When a word becomes too common, it loses its meaning. That is certainly the case with this one.

It was already true in 1973 when Eric Sloane wrote *The Spirits of '76* to prepare for the Bicentennial celebrations. So he begins his Chapter 9 with a reflection on the barns in America in the 18th century. They were huge and so were the houses, much larger than anything in the old world. The people strove to make them vast, much larger than was ever necessary.

He traces this to a fundamental American vision. We would replace the aristocracy of old, with barons and lords on landed estates, with a citizen-based meritocracy. We would all work our way toward becoming masters of our own domain. We would not need to be compliant and obedient subjects. We would all become kings of our own realm.

I think about this walking through nearly any American neighborhood in the suburbs. Europeans find the scene pretty funny. Everyone has a lawn. Each resident is charged with keeping it up and is judged by others if he fails. All of these are truly just European-style estates but in a miniature form. That is the cultural ideal in America.

Every man a king, goes the old phrase, and there is a lot of truth in it. At our founding, we left the idea of earthly kingship behind. If you read Thomas Paine, you will be startled by how much he rages against the monarchy, jeering at their privileges and clothing and power. It's pretty obvious that he despises monarchical government, and his contemporaries felt the same.

They felt like they had stumbled on an insight – that the people could rule themselves – and they were sticking with it, betting everything on it, and maniacally focused on proving the point. They did, and the new system worked for a very long time, so long as the idea of independence loomed large in the American frame of mind.

At some uncertain point, mostly in the 20th century, the idea of independence gave way to other ambitions: the plan, the empire, the systems, and the grand collective goal. This always comes down to one thing. More power to the state and less power to the individual. Independence as individuals and as a nation took a backseat to the collective dream. This has come at the expense of our liberty.

If we are to recapture the American Dream, and greatness along with it, we must revive the real meaning of independence. It means much more than having a home with a lawn, though that might be part of it. It means the ability to make decisions for yourself and your family without your peaceful wishes being overridden by bureaus and the designs of experts.

To value independence means trusting people to manage their own lives. That's not as easy as it may sound.

I wrote an article calling for an end to the Department of Education. I said that states, communities, and families could manage education on their own. I gave evidence from history and from existing data on expenditures versus outcomes.

A nice person wrote me an objection. How can we be sure that stupid will do what is right? Don't we need force and government power to get families and communities to teach the kids who otherwise would languish in ignorance and illiteracy?

I sent my correspondent some literature on the subject from American history along with some chatty discussion of homeschooling, hybrid schools, and community capacity for generating educational options.

It didn't matter. She kept coming back to the same theme: she just doesn't trust people and instead wants to force them. All the evidence of educational failure in the current system could not convince her. We had reached an impasse. She fundamentally distrusted the capacity of society to generate outcomes better than what she had dreamed up in her head that she would do by force.

At that point, I was at a loss as to how to convince her. She doubted the workability of independence. She didn't believe in freedom. There is simply no way to overcome such a view. I do think she could come around, but it is going to take much more than a text-based email conversation to do it. She needs to read, reflect, and rethink.

We all need to do this. As we look back on the Founding Fathers, we find a generation that feared and hated tyranny much more than they worried about the social consequences of freedom. None of them believed that freedom and independence would create utopia. But they did believe that freedom is the best system to guarantee against despotism and likely produces the best possible outcomes we can expect in a deeply flawed world.

Rallying around that insight, they set up a new system of government, and mapped out their philosophy for the ages. They explained in such detail because they knew they had a unique insight, and it would require explanation to make it stick. We need to revisit this explanation today in order to rediscover the meaning and intent.

At some point after the Cold War and perhaps much earlier, the idea of a global American empire took hold among the elites. It spilled over into every area: trade, culture, technology, and everything. These global institutions that emerged are not subject to any kind of plebiscite. The American people cannot control them. The billionaires and multinational foundations do.

Now comes the corrective. People want to put America first. That is because the people want to be in charge once again, in a way that is consistent with the promise of our heritage. We have to be able to vote for representatives, and they have to have power over the bureaucracy. If we do not have that, we do not have democracy. And we certainly don't have independence so long as the World Health Organization rules our bodies and the World Trade Organization runs our businesses.

Reclaiming independence means letting go of these global institutions and returning government to the people. That's a big ambition, much easier to say than achieve. But at least we are getting back on the right track. We've tried empire. We don't like it because it compromises our freedom and independence.

Again, the foundation of America is the Declaration of

Independence. Its signing is our birthday. It's more important than any other document in our history. It is known the world over. Its themes changed history. The world loves it. We should love it too. It should be the foundation of American life. All reforms for the future should look to it for guidance.

The Spirit of Awareness

The final chapter of Eric Sloane's *The Spirits of '76*, written to celebrate the 200th anniversary of America's founding, ends with a kind of sadness. This is in contrast to the feel of the opening of the book, which is more sprightly and hopeful. The last chapter doesn't leave much room for hope, and that is because of its unexpected subject matter.

He is speaking about what he calls awareness, by which he means the capacity of the individual fully to appreciate what is around him, his circumstances, his opportunities, and his thinking on himself, others, and the meaning of life. He is right: we hardly do this anymore.

The chapter begins by debunking the claim that solitude and silence are always regrettable. He sees solitude as the natural state, the best position in which a person can be in order to discover himself fully. He has a long screed about the complications, noises, and pointless busyness of modern life – in 1973!

Imagine if he could see today. Our phones never stop demanding our attention. We can hardly sit for drinks with friends and not have them bleeping, buzzing, and musicalizing constantly.

Here is something I just despise. I'll be having a conversation with friends. Someone asks a question like: when did the religious wars end? Someone grabs a phone and starts talking into it, and the answer comes instantly. We sit there all feeling stupid and strangely defeated. We are not happy to have the answer. We are sad that the flow was interrupted by a stupid piece of technology.

A friend of mine was very strict about this. He insisted on banning all phones in any setting where friends are talking: living rooms, dining halls, restaurants, or even on the street standing around in a circle. He hated them. Anyone who took out a phone in his presence got a ferocious earful.

I used to think he went too far. Maybe not. Maybe we all need to shape up. Do you check your phone at night? I admit that I do sometimes. I always regret it. It serves no point. Turn it off. There is no downside.

To Sloane's point, we surround ourselves with all this racket and interruption because we are afraid of ourselves and our solitude. We have fake friends, fake communities, fake urgencies, fake surprises, fake entertainments, fake everything. We seek to fill our lives with a nonstop stream of dopamine hits that only make us sad in the long run.

Sloane says he spent several weeks in solitude at a Vermont farmhouse, sitting by the fire, reading by candlelight, cooking his own food, listening to no music and having no guests. He described the feeling as fundamentally disorienting but in a good way. Ultimately, he says, it reset his entire mindset and life. He always looks back on those days as the ideal and tries to recreate them in his head.

Years ago, a priest invited me to a private retreat. I would live in a small room with no decorations. I would pray alone and with the community. I would eat in silence. I would not talk. I would only reflect.

As he described this, my answer came quickly: absolutely not. That sounds utterly terrible to me and I could never do it. I never looked back. But sometimes I wonder if I should have said yes. What precisely did I fear so much about solitude? What did I fear that I would find out about myself?

Aloneness goes with awareness. I'm more convinced than ever that there is no such thing as learning in a classroom or in a mass setting. All education is ultimately self-education, even if it can be hopefully directed by others. What we know, we learn by our own decisions, by discovering connections in our complicated minds, putting things together in ways that only happen in the solitary state of our own thought processes, uninterrupted.

The greatest blessing of my life came when my father rescued me from classes at a huge state university for which I was paying the bills with two jobs. My life was a mess, not because of partying or time wasting but because I never stopped doing things to survive. He found me a scholarship at a small liberal arts program and let me live in his house to reduce the financial burden.

I attended my classes with just 6-15 people and headed straight to the library. That was my home. I did reading for the classes and then went deeper. I read books in the footnotes, Then I read the books next to the books in the stakes (the elimination of library stacks is a tragedy). I got faster and faster and ever more curious about every topic imaginable.

At some point, I began to see the library as an impossible

world of infinite adventure, offering an infinity of thrills in book after book and page after page. I would gather 20 books around me and start reading and taking notes furiously, sticking with it until the library closed at 11pm each day. My eyes became so bloodshot that I got addicted to eye drops.

Never did I stop to think this was weird. I was falling in love with learning, with discovery, with ideas and the life of the mind. I was in a state of absolute solitude, a position of hyper-awareness. Nearly everything I know today came from those two years of deep embed. It was awareness. It changed me forever.

More precisely, I would say that most of what I think now has a foundation in those years. I'm surprised at how much I draw from that experience. I truly wish everyone could have that. Sadly no one ever will, unless you really do make your way to a monastery for years of study. They will probably be the last truly educated people on Earth.

In the end, we are alone. That is okay. That is good. It is an opportunity to be aware, to grow, to mature, to connect with ourselves and whatever lives in the eternal spaces of our imaginations. In solitude we find faith. In solitude we find truth. In solitude we find peace.

We lack all three in our times, and we have built the world this way. We have done this to prevent ourselves from finding out the truth about ourselves. This is tragic, and yet we will keep doing it even though our current path leaves us more lonely than ever.

Interestingly, Sloane stopped his book there until a friend said that he seemed to end on a hopeless note. So he wrote a last reflection simply called Hope. Does it exist? Yes, of course it does. In his view, the path to hope is found through reflection on the virtues of the American experience and the attempt to apply them in our times.

Honestly, today I feel much more hopeful than he must have felt in 1973. We have seen how the people can rise up and make change happen. We observe new interest in the founding documents, the American spirit, the truth about our lives, our liberties, and what must be done to recapture what we have lost.

The 250th anniversary of our founding is a great marker. Let's treat it as an inspiration to improve and repair our lives and our country, as a model for the world that it has always been.

The Spirit of Enterprise

In the 1990s and for years into our century, it was common to ridicule the government for being technologically backwards. We were all gaining access to fabulous things, including webs, apps, search tools, and social media. But governments at all levels were stuck in the past using IBM mainframes and large floppy disks. We had a great time poking fun at them.

I recall the days of thinking government would never catch up to the glories and might of the market itself. I wrote several books on it, full of techno-optimism.

The new tech sector had a libertarian ethos about it. They didn't care about the government and its bureaucrats. They didn't have lobbyists in Washington. They were the new technologies of freedom and didn't care much about the old analogue world of command and control. They would usher in a new age of people power.

Here we sit a quarter-century later with documented evidence that the opposite happened. The private sector collects the data that the government buys and uses as a tool of control. What is shared and how many people see it is a matter of algorithms agreed upon by a combination of government agencies, university centers, various nonprofits, and the companies themselves. The whole thing has become an oppressive blob.

Every major company that once stayed far away from Washington now owns a similar giant palace in or around D.C., and they collect tens of billions in government revenue. Government has now become a major customer, if not the main customer, of the services provided by the large social media and tech companies. They are advertisers but also massive purchasers of the main product too.

Amazon, Microsoft, and Google are the biggest winners of government contracts, according to a report from Tussel. Amazon hosts the data of the National Security Agency with a $10 billion contract, and gets hundreds of millions from other governments. We do not know how much Google has received from the US government, but it is surely a substantial share of the $694 billion the federal government hands out in contracts.

Microsoft also has a large share of government contracts. In 2023, the US Department of Defense awarded the Joint Warfighter Cloud Capability contract to Microsoft, Amazon, Google, and Oracle. The contract is worth up to $9 billion and provides the Department of Defense with cloud services. It's just the beginning. The Pentagon is looking for a successor plan that will be bigger.

Actually, we don't even know the full extent of this but it is gargantuan. Yes, these companies provide the regular consumer services but a main and even decisive customer is government itself. As a result, the old laughing stock line about backwards tech at government agencies is no more. Today government is a main purchaser of tech services and is a top driver of the AI boom too.

It's one of the best-kept secrets in American public life, hardly talked about at all by mainstream media. Most people still think of tech companies as free-enterprise rebels. It's not true.

The same situation of course exists for pharmaceutical companies. This relationship dates even further back in time and is even tighter to the point that there is no real distinction between the interests of the FDA/CDC and large pharmaceutical companies. They are one and the same.

In this framework, we might also tag the agricultural sector, which is dominated by cartels that have driven out family farms. It's a government plan and massive subsidies that determine what is produced and in what quantity. It's not because of consumers that your Coke is filled with a scary product called "high fructose corn syrup," why your candy bar and danish have the same, and why there is corn in your gas tank. This is entirely the product of government agencies and budgets.

In free enterprise, the old rule is that the customer is always right. That's a wonderful system sometimes called consumer sovereignty. Its advent in history, dating perhaps from the 16th century, represented a tremendous advance over the old guild system of feudalism and certainly a major step over ancient despotisms. It's been the rallying cry of market-based economics ever since.

What happens, however, when government itself becomes a main and even dominant customer? The ethos of private enterprise is thereby changed. No longer primarily interested in serving the general public, enterprise turns its attention to serving its powerful masters in the halls of the state, gradually weaving close relationships and forming a ruling class that becomes a conspiracy against the public.

This used to go by the name "crony capitalism," which perhaps describes some of the problems on a small scale. This is another level of reality that needs an entirely different name. That name is corporatism, a coinage from the 1930s and a synonym for fascism back before that became a curse word due to wartime alliances. Corporatism is a specific thing, not capitalism and not socialism but a system of private property ownership with cartelized industry that primarily serves the state.

The old binaries of the public and private sector – widely assumed by every main ideological system – have become so blurred that they no longer make much sense. And yet we are ideologically and philosophically unprepared to deal with this new world with anything like intellectual insight. Not only that, it can be extremely difficult even to tell the good guys from the bad guys in the news stream. We hardly know anymore for whom to cheer or boo in the great struggles of our time.

That's how mixed up everything has become. We've clearly traveled a long way from the 1970s!

Some might observe that this has been a problem far back in time. Starting with the Spanish-American War, we've seen a merger of public and private as involving the munitions industry.

This is true. Many Gilded Age fortunes were wholly legitimate and market-based enterprises but others were gathered from the nascent military-industrial complex that began to mature in the Great War and involved a vast range of industries from manufacturing to transportation to communications.

Of course in 1913, we saw the advent of a particularly egregious public-private partnership with the Federal Reserve, in which private banks merged into a unified front and agreed to service US government debt obligations in exchange for bailout guarantees. This monetary corporatism continues to vex us to this day, as does the military industrial complex.

How is it different from the past? It's different in degree and reach. The corporatist machine now manages the main products and services in our civilian life including the entire way we get information, how we work, how we bank, how we contact friends, and how we buy. It is the manager of the whole of our lives in every respect, and has become the driving force of product innovation and design. It has become a tool for surveillance in the most intimate aspects of our lives, including financial information and inclusive of listening devices we've willingly installed in our own homes.

In other words, this is no longer just about private companies providing the bullets and bombs for both sides in a foreign war and obtaining the rebuilding contracts after. The military-industrial complex has come home, expanded to everything, and invaded every aspect of our lives.

It has become a main curator and censor of our news and social media presence and postings. It is in a position to say which companies and products succeed and which ones fail.

It can kill apps in a flash if the well-placed person does not like what it is doing. It can order other apps to add or subtract to a blacklist based on political opinions. It can tell even the smallest company to comply or face death by lawfare. It can seize on any individual and make him a public enemy based entirely on an opinion or action that runs contrary to regime priorities.

In short, this corporatism – in all its iterations including the regulatory state and the patent war chest that maintains and enforces monopoly – is the core source of all the current despotism.

It obtained its first full trial run with the lockdowns of 2020, when tech companies and media joined in the ear-splitting propaganda campaigns to shelter in place, cancel holidays, and not visit grandma in the hospital and nursing home. It cheered as millions of small businesses were destroyed and big-box stores thrived as distributors of approved products, while vast swaths of the workforce were called nonessential and put on welfare.

This was the corporatist state at work, with a large corporate sector wholly acquiescent to regime priority and a government fully dedicated to rewarding its industrial partners in every sector that went along with the political priority at the moment. The trigger for the construction of the vast machinery that rules our lives was far back in time and always begins the same way: with a seemingly inauspicious government contract.

How well I recall those days in the 1990s when public schools first started to buy computers from Microsoft. Did alarm bells go off? Not for me. I had a typical attitude of any pro-business libertarian: whatever business wants to do, it should do. Surely it is up to the enterprise to sell to all willing buyers, even if that includes governments. In any case, how in the world would one prevent this? Government contracting with private business has been the norm from time immemorial. No harm done.

And yet it turns out that vast harm was done. This was just the beginning of what became one of the world's largest industries, far more powerful and decisive over industrial organization than old-fashioned producer-to-consumer markets. Adam Smith's "butcher, baker, and brewery" have been crowded out by the very business conspiracies against which he gravely warned. These gigantic for-profit and public trading corporations became the operational foundation of the surveillance-driven corporatist complex.

We are nowhere near coming to terms with the implications of this. It goes way beyond and fully transcends the old debates between capitalism and socialism. Indeed that is not what this is about. The focus on that might be theoretically interesting but it has little or no relevance to the current reality in which public and private have fully merged and intruded into every aspect of our lives, and with fully predictable results: economic decline for the many and riches for the few.

This is also why neither the left nor the right, nor Democrats or Republicans, nor capitalists or socialists, seem to be speaking clearly to the moment in which we live. The dominating force on both the national and global scene today is techno-corporatism that intrudes itself into our food, our medicine, our media, our information flows, our homes, and all the way down to the hundreds of surveillance tools that we carry around in our pockets.

I truly wish these companies were genuinely private but they are not. They are de facto state actors. More precisely, they all work hand-in-glove and which is the hand and which is the glove is no longer clear.

Coming to terms with this intellectually is the major challenge of our times. Dealing with it juridically and politically seems like a much more daunting task, to say the least. The problem is complicated by the drive to purge serious dissent at all levels of society. How did American capitalism become American corporatism? A little at a time and then all at once.

The Spirit of Physicality

The canoe in the backyard by the lake was upside down on dry land. I used it as a stepping stool to get to the other boat. My foot punched a hole, which rather mortified me because the boat belonged to my friend. I quickly discerned that now the boat could not be put in water. That much about boating I know.

Apologizing abjectly and ready to write a check to pay, he assured me that it is no biggie. The boat was already full of holes and useless. Still I was mortified because the experience taps into an insecurity I have. My biggest fear these days is that I'm not very good at the real world.

That was a dumb mistake. It's all part of getting used to real life again following the lockdown years that coincided with mass adoption of digital technology made vastly more addictive and seemingly indispensable with AI and the QRing of everything.

Nowadays, many of us are looking for every opportunity to reconnect to the physical world. Once we were on the other canoe paddling around in the lake, I could feel the psychological decompression taking place. Just hearing the water lap up against the side of the boat and observing the trees on the bank was lovely. The mind wanders in wonderful ways.

It sure beats screen time. Let's just say that boating in the metaverse is a poor substitute.

In many ways, the digital world was always a trick, even a lie. It is useful, like any tool, but hardly a replacement. This much is now obvious to most of us.

A year or so ago, I did a bit of a mental experiment on this. What if we really did as a society entirely migrate to the cloud? It seems superficially plausible for some classes of workers, and they were riding high during the lockdown years. But consider what we would be missing.

Food is one example. There are several bakeries in town that I like to visit. Just sitting there watching them at work, making breads and pies and cakes, you realize that this would be impossible to do without genuine physical skills. That is a beautiful thing.

The same is true of the butchers, brewers, and gardeners in town. They live and breathe the physical world. I'm more appreciative than ever before of such professions, and that includes the cellist, the plumber, the guy who specializes in wallpaper installations, the actors on stage, the people who keep the stores stocked, and so on.

There is a romance associated with the non-migratory physical world. It keeps us bound to reality, and immune to the hideous claim that real life can be replaced by screen time.

I personally draw the line at using my phone to pull up a restaurant menu. Never! If there is no printed menu, I will ask someone to tell me what's available. If that doesn't work, I will just order a hamburger. Regardless, I'm personally done with "touchless" menus and all they represent.

After years of pushing for computers in the classroom, teachers and administrators these days are working furiously to reverse their errors. They are banning devices in the classroom.

They are teaching kids from physical books and insisting on penmanship.

At concerts and theaters, you see more and more venues bagging phones with timed locks to prevent customers from pulling them out during the performance. The time when loudspeakers beg people to turn them off is over. We are moving to the point of zero tolerance for this nonsense.

It's the same with private dinner parties. There are no stated rules but I've noticed a huge change. I always try to keep my phone out of sight and out of mind but sometimes in a lull I've taken it out and got a quick look. I can feel the stares of disapproval. This is as it should be. You are either present or you are not. If you would prefer screen time to a dinner party, stay home!

A leading challenge for all parents now is not teaching kids "computer literacy" but throttling screen time. Many have just said no to all digital devices before the age of 15. That's not entirely realistic for most people. After all, every parent of young kids knows that the iPad is the single greatest babysitting device ever invented. It's nearly impossible to resist.

That said, any parent who permits kids unmitigated access to the Internet these days is insane. No responsible parent would do it. These days, parents keep very strict controls on what sites are available, automatic timed shutdowns, and more besides. It takes some technological sophistication to set it up and it is essential.

More and more I meet people who are eschewing digital tech

in as much of their lives as possible. They have home theaters that only showed DVDs. The popularity of long-playing records seems to be on the increase. Homes without any television seem more common.

The rejection of all the latest gizmos seems almost to be a class marker, proof that you are a real person who is hip to the game and rejects it. I cannot remember the last time I saw anyone yelling at their home assistant to play a particular piece of music, for example.

Part of this trend is not just the rejection but the embrace of the real with newfound love of hiking, physical books, traveling, jogging on open roads, focus on wellness and physical health generally, love of sunshine, and so on. It's absolutely crazy that we nearly forgot about all these things.

If you think back to the spring of 2020, the World Economic Forum put out a book soon after lockdowns came to the world. It was called *The Great Reset*. It was a puffed-up and pompous little manifesto. It was widely misunderstood. The plot in the book had nothing to do with socialism. It was all about a full and global industrial reset. The core idea was to force a shift from physical to digital industry, from machinery to keyboards, from steel and iron to glass screens, all in the name of efficiency, surveillance, and hygiene.

Think of this historically. We went through another big change in industrial structure in the last quarter of the 19th century, as agriculture gave way to the urban factory setting. Instead of letting it happen organically, it was forced on many people in many lands. After the Bolshevik Revolution, Lenin could not think of anything better to do with his newfound power than to attempt the forced electrification of Russia.

To dream of converting whole societies from one dominant technology to another is the stuff of tyrants' dreams. This is essentially what happened with the 20-year-long efforts over "global warming" that mutated into a general concern over "climate change" as if climates don't change normally. The state was marshaled somehow to manage the climate/weather or whatever. Crazy stuff.

The "Great Reset" was more of the same. And the lockdowns over a virus had that very industrial ambition, to force us all into digital dependency and addiction. It was bad for health and bad for life.

Now that we are onto the game, we are moving toward active resistance. By all means, let's use digital technology to better human life but not control and ruin it, which it is certainly doing now. We need all in our own lives to seriously rethink and rediscover what we have left behind, whether that is cooking, gardening, playing music, reading physical books, or simply hopping in a canoe and paddling around a lake.

Simple things. Beautiful things. Physical things.

The Spirit of Localism

For most meat buyers, the product is pre-cut, wrapped up in plastic, priced, and sitting there in a cabinet at a well-lit store as a finished product. That's how people buy their meat. They don't know any other way. It's a habit and hard to break. It seems like a pre-cooked version of pre-packaged food, sanitized and far removed from its source.

But in other parts of the country, there are still some meat shops with professional butchers. I'm fortunate enough to have about 6 in a 5-mile radius of where I live. In my experience, the product you obtain from a local butcher is another level of excellence. This applies to the steaks, the sausages, the minced beef, and everything else. The butcher is the way to go, if you can find one.

Such shops will typically be more expensive, but the difference is worth it. It's hard convincing people of that these days, especially given the price increases over four years and the sharp declines in household real income. It seems instead that this is the time to save money.

As a result, most local butcher shops have taken a serious hit. They were closed down during Covid and they opened to a world of consumers desperate to save money. Still, they are keeping on and maintaining high standards.

I personally adore the butcher shop and all the conversations that can be had here about meats, feeds, processing, seasonality, and so on. It's all so fascinating. Typically in such places, you will be able to carry on a conversation with the man who actually takes the meat from huge animal parts into saleable units, including the operation of the scary bone cutters and extremely sharp knives.

To see the product go from carcass to your grill grants a new appreciation of the fullness and reality of what it takes to feed the human person. It's not just a store but a process, and not just a company but real people with real skill.

The whole history of eating is bound up with the legend of the butcher, which appears in literature as far back as language exists. The key has always been about owning the tools. Time was when they were rare and much sought after.

My own great-great grandfather moved to Texas from Massachusetts and opened up a blacksmith shop around 1830. He had the only one in town and sold all the tools to the local butchers but of course also to the doctors and surgeons. They were often the same people, giving rise to the profession called the butcher-surgeon, which is a scary thought.

His son was a young man and a worker at the blacksmith shop when Texas found itself dragged into the Civil War to fight for a nation it had only recently (and reluctantly) joined. So when he was drafted by the Confederate army, he took the role in the unit for which he was naturally suited. He became the medic. Why? The answer is simple: he had the tools for sawing off limbs and otherwise cutting people up as need be. No, he had no medical training but such were the days.

The famed opera *Barber of Seville* by Rossini gives more context to the implication of owning the tools. He was not just a barber but a dentist. He would pull teeth and cut hair on the same visit. The delivery of love letters and arranging of trysts was just a side gig given to a trusted member of the community who commonly entered private spaces in people's homes.

See what happens when you have the right tools? You might start as the blacksmith but you end up as the barber, the surgeon, the dentist, and the deliverer of secret notes, all made possible by owning pliers, saws, and knives. That's the way the old world worked, long before tools became a widely available commercial product and people could specialize.

In any case, back to the butcher. It's fascinating to discuss their occupation with them and discern the pride they take in their sausages, meat slices, and otherwise. They absolutely know what is what, and it's an absolute joy to learn from them about the best cuts of the day. None of this is available at regular supermarkets.

It's often true that local butchers source their meat from local ranchers and are fussier about the location of processing plants. They care because they know that people who are happy with what they sell will come back. They can do custom cuts based on your description and make just the right standing rib roast for your party, plus explain the best way to prepare it.

In meats, there are always seasonal offerings, even if the superstore pretends otherwise. The freshness of the product really does matter, as you will quickly discover once you plunge into this world.

Remember going to an amazing Italian restaurant and slicing

through the perfect tender sausage? Every time you snag a packet from the grocery store, it fails to turn out that way, no matter how you cook it. This is often because the casing is artificial and the meat itself is packed too tightly due to industrial methods. Get the same thing from a local butcher and you find yourself back in the high-end restaurant with the perfect dish.

You can also learn something. Like everyone else these days, I became truly fixated on the issue of grain-fed vs grass-fed beef, fussily preferring the latter. A butcher recently explained to me the tradeoffs of this preference. The more the cow wanders around eating grass, the less fat is built up and the leaner the product. That can be great but there is also a case for grass-fed and grain-finished beef. He sells what you want but he has a point about the flavor tradeoffs, and convinced me not to fuss over topics about which I know next to nothing.

In any case, to me the true feeling of excitement comes from a sense that I'm buying my meat the same way my grandfather and his father before him, going back many generations, bought their meat. It's like supporting a wonderful tradition, and saving at least one profession from becoming extinct and impersonal in the hyper-industrialized world of centralization and impersonal forces.

And need I point out the not-so-quiet war ongoing against meat itself? It should be obvious to you. There's never been a better time to make it clear: humans are meat eaters and we will remain so as long as we care about health! Nor are bugs a good substitute.

Adam Smith famously wrote: “It is not from the benevolence of the butcher, the brewer, or the baker that we expect our dinner, but from their regard to their own interest.”

Indeed, there is no problem in showing a bit of benevolence back, if only to break the superstore habit. You might find as I did that the service and product are more than worth the difference.

The Spirit of Forbearance

Bleary-eyed and confused, we awakened with the cock crow at 4:30 am, if memory serves. Seemed like the middle of the night to me. It's one thing to wake early to catch a flight, but to start a day of hard physical work?

It was the one time in my life that, at the age of 20, I spent two days on a farm living with an actual farm family, doing farm things. The memory of those two days – from the struggle, the exhaustion, the food, and mostly the sense of time that is part of the agrarian life – has stuck with me ever since.

We can all learn from how farmers manage their time and lives.

In this case, the work began right away as the dawn was barely appearing. I recall feeding the chickens, doing something with pigs, and bailing hay but walking through stunning amounts of cow waste to get there. Then we headed to the horses to water and brush them. Then out to the pastures and hopping on big trucks to do something I cannot recall.

All of this happened before 8 am, by which time I was hungrier than I can ever recall being. Breakfast was gigantic with pancakes, biscuits, bacon, ham, eggs, strangely bitter greens, and coffee and juices, and people ate like I've never seen. I did too.

We stood up from the table and headed out again to pick up where we left off, on trucks, tending to the land, chasing animals here and there, fussing over crops, poking around on fences, securing and fixing things.

Then lunch came, and it was small but in the middle of it, a varmint appeared outside. The father grabbed his gun and shot it from the living room window, making an enormous explosion to which no one paid much attention.

What struck me then was the patience, the deliberation, the absence of frustration, the sense of duty, the focus on completing a job, and the way in which the position of the sun more than the clock seemed to determine what happened when.

The fence was broken, for example. It needed to be fixed. The nail bent and broke. It needed to be pulled. A new screw was needed. Found one in the barn. The wood was warped and weathered. Cut a new one, shape it, nail it in place.

Watching this unfold, and a thousand other things that day that seemed to go wrong, I came to realize something. This farm, this estate, this family, did not regard breakage as an abnormal occurrence. It was a main driver of life, something that calls forth all our efforts on a continuing basis.

Fixing broken things, adapting when stuff does not go exactly as planned, was not just something you do; it was the essence of the job of life itself. That's all we do: fix things. Adapt. Keep moving forward through every exigency and barrier.

Having been swept away by the writings and life work of Eric Sloane, collector, and illustrator, I've been thinking often about his outlook. Among his fascinating insights concerns how we use time.

He has this passage in which he celebrates the pacing of the farmer, the most experienced worker with the biggest range of skills and the longest uninterrupted traditions. The farmer approaches time as a gift and his use of it as something to treasure and treat with care.

It is never about rushing, panicking, getting angry at things, or otherwise regretting the existence of toil. It is about embracing the limits and opportunities of the world around you as it exists, and viewing one's job as a patient, deliberate, and respectful undertaking of one's duties. You just do what you must do, completely and wholly, one step at a time.

This is pretty much the opposite of how our age has trained our brains. Anything we have to do we are told to regret, and always seek out some shortcut or technology to do it for us. We are suckers for idiotic things like apps to turn on lights and machines that do our thinking for us. Anything to reduce the toil and tedium, take away the tasks, and be "smart" so that we don't have to be.

This is about an attitude toward life. We are forever kvetching and complaining about anything that takes time or requires effort. What is it that we are seeking to do instead? That's never quite clear. Once we find ourselves doing the thing we think we would rather do, it turns out that this too becomes an arduous task and grates on us and leads to kvetch some more.

It never ends, such that our whole lives consist of nothing but complaints. You think this has a bleeding effect on our minds, bodies, and souls? It certainly does. It leads to relentless decay, a draining of all joy from the course of regular life.

Then people turn to substances and drugs to make the pain go away, except that this only makes it worse. Then we add more and more until the whole of life is utterly miserable. We come to regret and curse physicality itself, which opens other pathologies.

My theory is that this is why all the technologies that are supposed to make us happier have done the opposite. It's because the demand for them is rooted in the promotion of discontent. Once that attitude of universal dissatisfaction with one's plight overwhelms any joy we might take in achievement, no product and no substance can repair the damage.

Let's look at a practical example. In every kitchen, there will come a time when you or someone drops a glass on the floor. It breaks and shatters. What happens next is telling.

In a suburban home where all tasks are annoying and all breakage is an existential disruption, the breaking of a glass in the kitchen might lead to a great drama, anger, hectoring of the causal agent, and a sense of trauma all around, following by a huffy cleanup punctuated by curses and grave frustration.

In the farmer household, in contrast, nothing much is said. One gets the broom and dustpan and sweeps it up. There are no recriminations, curses to the heavens, anger at getting a new one, and so on. There is just an awareness that breakage is part of life.

Which is the better approach? Once the glass hits the floor and breaks, nothing can be done to reverse that history. It is done, already in the past. What matters now is how one responds to it.

Herein is the test. A person who can approach that scene with an attitude of quiet dignity, using time and tools to undertake the necessary cleaning, is likely to be a happier person overall.

This is because the breaking of the glass is a metaphor for the stream of life. The course of time itself is nothing but a relentless toggle between building and breaking, progress and regress, creativity and crashing. One goes with the other and the downsides need not be treated as a horrid interruption but an opportunity to deploy skills in a different way, an opportunity to make good use of our hands, legs, bodies, and minds.

This is all about habit formation. Back to the kitchen for guidance. Notice that many people love to cook but few like to clean. In the farmer's kitchen, relatively sparse with few machines other than a toaster and blender, cooking and cleaning go together in one motion. Always cleaning while cooking to the point that when the meal is served, the kitchen is orderly already.

It's in the urban kitchen of the perpetually disgruntled, large, and packed with plugged-in gizmos and expensive machines that you find the stacks of pans, sinks full of tools, and grime everywhere. Everything is dirty. This is because of the mental habit of always regarding the arduous task as the exception, the interruption, the regrettable thing that should be done by an app or a servant but certainly not ourselves.

In Sloane's view, the key to a happy life is simply to emulate the farmer. Do what needs to be done, without frustration, regret, rush, complaint, or childish protest, but instead with patience and awareness. If we can somehow learn to love the gift of time and use it with diligence and discipline, we can gradually reformulate how we think about the purpose of our life.

My day on the farm introduced me to a different pace and path of life, one I thought I would leave behind when I moved far away. Now it is easier to see: the life and values of the farmer are worthy of emulation in every profession and path of life.

The farmer expects breakage and deals with it with diligence and persistence. So it is with American ideals. They break. They must be restored. To do so requires the forbearance of a land owner working for generations to make a better life for himself and his progeny. The American experiment has made us all landowners and stakeholders in the ideals for which this great country was founded.

A final question for us and our country: do we merely exist day to day – dreading our lot, feeding disgruntlement, waiting for its end – or do we aspire to create a better future? There is a foundational difference in these two ways of thinking and being. Merely existing means caring nothing for principles. Building a brighter future for ourselves and those who follow us must necessarily study and take recourse to the past – its values, its ideals, its practical realization – as the basis on which we live, work and decide what that future is.

About Brownstone Institute

Brownstone Institute, established May 2021, is a publisher and research institute that places the highest value on the voluntary interaction of individuals and groups while minimizing the use of violence and force, including that which is exercised by public authority.

www.ingramcontent.com/pod-product-compliance
Lightning Source LLC
LaVergne TN
LVHW051008080826

845145LV00009B/2518

* 9 7 8 1 6 3 0 6 9 3 0 1 5 *